# From Seed to Seed

## The Mighty Oak Tree

By Margaret Williamson

Discover Plants and Animals
Vowel Teams
(oa, oe, ow)

Scan this code to access the Teacher's Notes for this series or visit
www.norwoodhousepress.com/decodables

NORWOOD HOUSE PRESS

**DEAR CAREGIVER**, *The Decodables* series contains books following a systematic, cumulative phonics scope and sequence aligned with the science of reading. Each book allows its reader to apply their phonics knowledge in engaging and relatable texts. The words within each text have been carefully selected to ensure that readers can rely on their decoding skills as they encounter new or unfamiliar words. They also include high frequency words appropriate for the target skill level of the reader.

When reading these books with your child, encourage them to sound out words that are unfamiliar by attending to the target letter(s) and sounds. If the unknown word is an irregularly spelled high frequency word or a word containing a pattern that has yet to be taught (challenge words) you may encourage your child to attend to the known parts of the word and provide the pronunciation of the unknown part(s). Rereading the texts multiple times will allow your child the opportunity to build their reading fluency, a skill necessary for proficient comprehension.

You can be confident you are providing your child with opportunities to build their decoding abilities which will encourage their independence as they become lifelong readers.

Happy Reading!

Emily Nudds, M.S. Ed Literacy
Literacy Consultant

Norwood House Press • www.norwoodhousepress.com
The Decodables ©2024 by Norwood House Press. All Rights Reserved.
Printed in the United States of America.
367N–082023

Library of Congress Cataloging-in-Publication Data has been filed and is available at https://lccn.loc.gov/2023010455

Literacy Consultant: Emily Nudds, M.S.Ed Literacy
Editorial and Production Development and Management: Focus Strategic Communications Inc.
Editors: Christine Gaba, Christi Davis-Martell
Photo Credits: Shutterstock: Aleksander Bolbot (p. 19), Almgren (p. 10), Andrew Sabai (p. 6), Auhustsinovich (p. 17), charl898 (p. 21), Dan4Earth (p. 13), Evgen.Adamovich (p. 9), Fedorov Oleksiy (p. 8), Havryliuk-Kharzhevska (p. 18), Jessob (p. 9), Josh brown photography (p. 11), Jurgal (p. 17), Kazakova Maryia (p. 13), kristof lauwers (p. 12), k_samurkas (p. 17), Laurent CHEVALLIER (p. 8), Lightboxx (p. 21), Lubos Chlubny (cover, p. 15), Macrovector (covers), Mark Green (p. 20), Mike Ver Sprill (p. 4), Mircea Costina (p. 14), PHOTO FUN (p. 16), Red monkey (p. 5), Smileus (p. 7), tamu1500 (p. 9).

Hardcover ISBN: 978-1-68450-690-3    Paperback ISBN: 978-1-68404-900-4
eBook ISBN: 978-1-68404-955-4

# Contents

# A Symbol of Strength

The oak tree is of great importance. It stands for strength and wisdom.

This live oak, named Angel Oak, is thought to be between 400 and 500 years old.

Many states in the United States boast of the beautiful oak tree as their symbol.

The Connecticut Old Oak is a symbol of freedom.

# The Majestic Oak

Oak trees grow tall and wide. They are strong and solid. They live between 200 and 1,000 years. There are more than 500 kinds of oak trees. They grow all over the world.

There are many bur oaks in Iowa.

Most oak trees lose their leaves in the fall.

They are known as a thirsty tree. Oak trees can soak up 50 gallons of water every day.

Oak leaves are long and wide. They have a wobbly shape that looks like long toes. The oak leaf stem is short.

This photo shows an oak leaf.

A pin oak has thinner leaves.

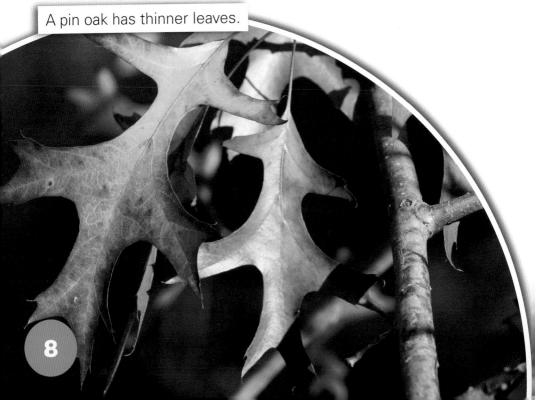

Live oaks can grow very big.

Some oaks are known to drop their leaves before the snow. Some are **evergreens**, like the live oak and the bamboo-leaf oak. They keep their leaves.

Fallen oak leaves coat the ground.

The Bamboo-leaf oak does not lose its leaves in the fall.

# Oak Trees Have Flowers?

Oak trees have male and female flowers. They grow together on the same branch. They are called oak **catkins**. Willow trees also have catkins. Unlike some other plants though, oak flowers do not grow to be big and full of color.

Oak flowers in the spring.

The yellow pollen glows in the sun.

The male flowers hang low on the tree branches. They are filled with yellow pollen. They look like a fuzzy caterpillar with a yellow **cloak**.

The female flowers are very small and red. They grow high up on the branch.

You must look up to see the small red flowers.

When the wind blows, the pollen floats and **fertilizes** the female flowers. An acorn begins to grow. A seed is inside the acorn. When the acorn drops from the tree, the seed begins to grow on its own.

An oak seed grows from the acorn.

An oak tree takes many years to grow.

# From Acorn to Mighty Oak

An acorn is the fruit of an oak tree. Acorns don't look like fruit. They look more like a nut. The acorn has a very hard shell. It is coated with **tannic acid**. This **acid** has a bitter taste. It helps protect the seed from some **foes**. It gives the seed inside the acorn time to grow.

Squirrels like acorns.

# FUN FACT

A doe can eat an acorn but a goat should not. The tannic acid coating on a green acorn can make some animals very sick.

Deer will eat oak leaves and acorns.

The seed inside the acorn grows slowly. The soil acts like a pillow. It also keeps the acorn warm and gives it water.

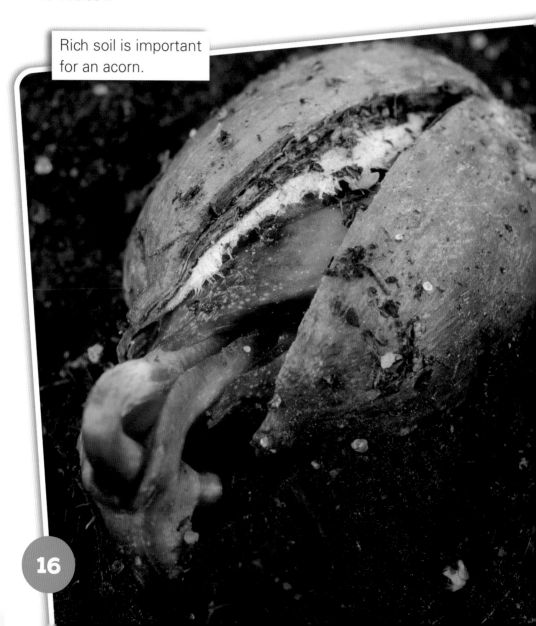

Rich soil is important for an acorn.

One oak tree can make about 2,000 acorns every year.

Acorns can cluster on an oak tree.

We see lots of acorns in the fall.

As the oak seed **germinates**, it grows a shoot. The shoot will grow a few leaves. The leaves need the sun's glow. Then the plant can start to make its own food. This is called **photosynthesis**.

A small oak can make its own food.

17

The **seedling** becomes a **sapling** when it is three feet tall. It takes over 20 years to grow into an adult oak tree. When the oak catkins show, the cycle of life will follow.

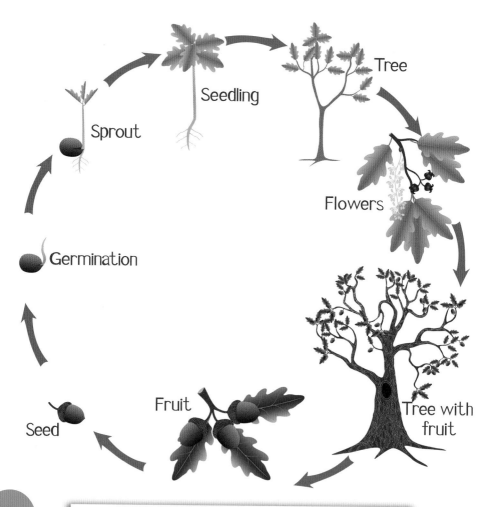

Sprout

Seedling

Tree

Flowers

Germination

Seed

Fruit

Tree with fruit

This diagram shows the life cycle of an oak tree.

This oak is decomposing.

As an oak tree dies, it **decomposes**. Its goal is to fertilize the soil for its fellow trees.

# Famous Oaks

The Great Oak is a very old and sacred oak tree in the United States. It is on the Pechanga (pə-**chon**-gə) Reserve. That is on the west coast. It is known to be over 1,000 years old. The Great Oak is 100 feet tall and 20 feet wide. The branches are low to the ground.

Major Oak in Sherwood Forest in England is over 1,000 years old, too. This is the forest where Robin Hood and his Merry Men used to roam.

Poles are used to help hold up Major Oak's very heavy branches so they don't break off.

# Solid and Strong

Oak is a hard wood. It is used to make loads of things. Furniture is made with oak wood. It is used to build boats. Some drums are made from oak wood. Oak wood makes strong floors that can take heavy loads.

This oak table is over 400 years old.

Oak trees are mighty in many ways. They live for hundreds of years. Under their shadow, small plants can grow. Birds know they are safe in oak branches. The acorns of oaks feed the wildlife that roam in the woods. They are an important part of a forest habitat.

## FUN FACT

Oak leaf symbols are sewn onto the uniforms of some **military** officers.

This is a military oak leaf cluster.

# Glossary

**acid** (ăs-ĭd): a sour-tasting liquid that can be harmful

**catkins**: the male flowers of the oak tree

**cloak**: a long, flowing cape with a hood

**decomposes** (dē-k əm-pōz- ĕs): broken down into smaller parts

**evergreens** (ĕv-ər-grēns): trees that stay green all year long

**fertilizes**: causes a new being to develop

**foes**: another word for enemies

**germinates** (jər-mĭn-āts): process of a seed turning into a sprout

**military** (mĭl-ə-tār-ē): people in the Army, Air Force, Navy, Marines, Space Force, or Coast Guard

**photosynthesis** (fō-tō-sĭn-thə-sĭs): the process by which green plants use sunlight to make their own food

**sapling**: a young tree

**seedling**: a young plant grown from a seed

**tannic acid**: a coating around the acorn

# Index

## Vowel Teams

| oa | | | oe | ow | | |
|---|---|---|---|---|---|---|
| boats | coating | loads | doe | blows | known | slowly |
| cloak | floats | oak | foes | follow | low | snow |
| coast | goal | roam | toes | glow | own | willow |
| coated | goat | soak | | grow(s) | show | yellow |
| | | | | know | | |

## High-Frequency Words

| | | | | | |
|---|---|---|---|---|---|
| animals | great | over | should | too | world |
| before | live | same | small | very | years |
| gives | old | | | | |

## Challenging Words

| | | | | | |
|---|---|---|---|---|---|
| beautiful | every | fruit | importance | officers | symbols |
| cycle | floors | heavy | known | sacred | thirsty |
| dies | food | high | mighty | strength | together |